Make·In·A Mug Recipes

Just mix it up in a cup, heat & serve!

Make In A Mug Recipes
©Product Concept Mfg., Inc.

Creative, tasty, fun...That's how people will describe these clever ideas, made up right in a mug. You'll find great recipes for one-dish meals, perfect for college students, singles, and seniors; fun snacks and desserts; and thoughtful ways to celebrate a birthday, thank a teacher, support a hardworking administrative assistant or new mom, and more!

Just make it up in a cup...
heat and eat!

Note that the microwave times given for these recipes are for making one mug. If making two or more mugs, they should be microwaved separately. Please be certain the mug is safe for oven or microwave.

Table of Contents

Table of Contents

Breakfast & Brunch Mugs

THREE CHEESE QUICHE

Ingredients:
1 egg
2 Tbsp milk
1/2 piece of French bread
2 tsp cream cheese, softened
1 Tbsp Cheddar cheese, finely shredded
1 Tbsp Swiss cheese, finely shredded
1/2 slice ham, chopped into small pieces
Salt and pepper to taste

Directions:
Beat egg and milk together with a fork in a mug. Remove the crust from the bread and tear bread into dime-size pieces, stir into the egg and milk. Add cheeses and ham, stir to combine. Microwave on high until done, about 1 minute, 20 seconds (time will vary depending on strength of the microwave). Add salt and pepper to taste.

Breakfast & Brunch Mugs

SIMPLY SCRAMBLED EGGS

Ingredients:
1 egg
2 Tbsp milk
1/2 Hawaiian dinner roll or other soft bread

Directions:
Whisk together the egg and the milk. Tear the roll into small pieces and put into the mug. Pour the egg mixture over the bread. Cook on high in the microwave until egg is done (times will vary depending on the microwave), about 1 minute, 20 seconds. Salt and pepper to taste.

RASPBERRY MUFFIN

Ingredients:
1/4 cup flour
Dash of salt
1 Tbsp sugar
1/4 tsp baking powder
2 Tbsp milk
1 small egg
1/4 tsp vanilla
1 Tbsp butter, melted
1/4 cup fresh or frozen raspberries

Directions:
Preheat oven to 400°. Spray the inside of an oven-proof mug with non-stick cooking spray. Combine the flour, salt, sugar, and baking powder. In a small bowl, whisk together the milk, egg, vanilla, and butter. Add the flour mixture to the milk mixture, stirring just to combine. In another bowl, mash the raspberries with a fork and then stir into the batter. Pour the batter into a mug. Bake in the oven for 15-20 minutes or until a toothpick inserted in the center comes out clean.

Breakfast & Brunch Mugs

OVERNIGHT FRENCH TOAST

Ingredients:
Leftover French bread (day old)
1 egg
1/2 cup half and half
1 tsp sugar
Dash of salt
Dash of cinnamon
Dash of nutmeg
1/8 tsp vanilla
1 Tbsp butter
Maple syrup

Directions:
Spray inside of an oven-proof mug with non-stick cooking spray. Tear bread into small pieces (no crusts), and put into the mug. In a bowl, whisk together the egg, half and half, sugar, salt, spices, and vanilla. Pour over the bread. Cover with foil and refrigerate overnight. In the morning, preheat oven to 350°. Remove the foil. Slice the butter into 3 pats and put on the top of the bread. Bake uncovered for 35 minutes or until bread is lightly browned. Pour maple syrup over the top before serving.

⠿⠿⠿ Breakfast & Brunch ⠿⠿⠿
Mugs

BACON AND EGG OMELET

Ingredients:
2 slices of bacon, cooked and cut into pieces
1 scallion, chopped
2 Tbsp milk
2 eggs
2 Tbsp Cheddar cheese, shredded

Directions:
Cook the bacon in the microwave until done. Put the bacon
and scallion into the mug. Whisk together the milk and eggs
and pour into the mug. Microwave on high for about 1 minute
or until eggs are nearly set. Sprinkle cheese on top and finish
cooking eggs. Salt and pepper to taste.

Breakfast & Brunch Mugs

BLUEBERRY-CINNAMON OATMEAL

Ingredients:
1/2 cup oats
1 Tbsp brown sugar
1/8 tsp cinnamon
1 egg
1/2 cup milk
1/4 cup blueberries

Toppings:
1/4 teaspoon cinnamon mixed with
1 Tbsp white sugar
Yogurt (optional)

Directions:
Spray the inside of a mug with non-stick cooking spray. Combine the first 5 ingredients in the mug, then gently fold in blueberries. Microwave for 2-3 minutes (depending on the strength of the microwave). Top with a sprinkle of cinnamon-sugar and a dollop of yogurt if desired.

⬛ Breakfast & Brunch ⬛ Mugs

MEXICAN EGGS

Ingredients:
1/4 cup cottage cheese
1 egg, beaten
1 Tbsp green chiles, drained
1/2 cup Monterey Jack cheese, shredded
2 tsp flour
1/2 Tbsp butter, melted
1/8 tsp baking powder

Toppings:
Sour cream
Salsa

Directions:
Preheat oven to 400°. Spray the inside of an oven-proof mug with non-stick cooking spray. Combine all ingredients, stirring together in the mug. Bake in the oven for 10-12 minutes or until eggs are set but not overcooked. Serve with sour cream and salsa.

Breakfast & Brunch
Mugs

PANCAKE IN A MUG

Ingredients:
1 cup pancake mix
1/4 cup milk
1/4 cup applesauce

Toppings:
Butter, melted
Syrup, warmed

Directions:
Spray a large mug with non-stick cooking spray. Mix the first three ingredients in a small bowl and then pour into the mug. Cook in a microwave for 1-2 minutes (depending on the strength of the microwave) or until done. Using a wooden skewer, poke holes in the hot pancake and pour the butter and syrup over the top until saturated.

⋯⋯ Breakfast & Brunch ⋯⋯
Mugs

WARM HONEY GRANOLA

Ingredients:

1 Tbsp butter	1 Tbsp wheat germ
1 Tbsp honey	1/8 tsp salt
1 Tbsp brown sugar	1/4 tsp cinnamon
1/2 cup rolled oats	1/4 tsp allspice
1 Tbsp nuts or sunflower seeds	

Toppings:
Yogurt and Fruit

Directions:
Combine in a mug the butter, honey, and brown sugar and heat in microwave for 1 minute until melted, stirring to combine. Add the rest of the dry ingredients and spices. Mix completely and cook again on high for 1 minute. Let sit for a minute then serve warm with yogurt and fruit.

Heaven knows how much you're appreciated! But do you?

With recipes like these, you can get creative and make up a healthy "good morning" mug for a hardworking teacher, volunteer, or co-worker. For Warm Honey Granola: mix all the dry ingredients in the perfect mug. Drizzle honey over, and top with a pat of butter. Cover well with plastic wrap. Secure in a package with a small container of yogurt and choice of fruit (apple, banana, raisins). Add a note with instructions on microwaving...and, most importantly, your words of appreciation.

Breakfast & Brunch
Mugs

DUTCH APPLE PANCAKE

Ingredients:
2 Tbsp butter
1 egg
1/4 cup milk
1/4 cup flour
Apple slices
Maple syrup

Directions:
Preheat oven to 425°. Melt butter in a large fat-bottomed mug, then swirl the butter to coat the sides of the mug. Using a mixer, mix the eggs in a separate bowl for 1 minute. Add the milk and then gradually add the flour. Blend for 30 seconds. Pour into the mug with the melted butter. Bake in oven for 15 minutes or until puffy and golden brown. Put apples in the center of the pancake. Drizzle with syrup before serving.

CINNAMON BUTTER QUINOA

Ingredients:
1/4 cup quinoa
1/2 cup cold water
1/8 tsp cinnamon
2 tsp butter

For Cinnamon Butter:
2 Tbsp butter, at room temperature
1 Tbsp light brown sugar
1/8 tsp ground cinnamon

Milk or cream, to taste

Directions:
Rinse quinoa in a colander with cool water. Drain quinoa and put into a mug. Stir in cold water, cinnamon and 2 tsp butter. Microwave on high for 4 minutes. Stir and microwave 3 more minutes. Remove from microwave, cover and let sit for 2 minutes. Stir. Serve with cinnamon butter and milk.

Quinoa is called the "super grain" because it contains more protein than any other grain. Gluten-free, and packed with health benefits, this is a thoughtful dish to make for the health-conscious, and will especially be appreciated by those who are gluten-sensitive.

Chili, Chowder & Soup Mugs

SWEET AND SPICY CHILI

Ingredients:

1/4 cup ground beef, cooked and crumbled	2 tsp chili seasoning
	1-2 tsp molasses
1 Tbsp kidney beans	1 tsp brown sugar
1 Tbsp chili beans	1/2 tsp cumin
1 Tbsp corn	1/4 cup tomato sauce
1 Tbsp diced tomatoes	1/4 cup beef broth

Directions:

Place all ingredients in a soup mug and cook in a microwave on high for 1 1/2 minutes or until hot. Serve with corn chips, cheese, and a dollop of sour cream.

Having fans over to watch the big game?

Make up a few of these mugs so everyone can top off their chili mug as they choose. Get in the spirit by serving in team logo mugs. And if one of your guests happens to be having a birthday, send the birthday person home with their own team mug as a reminder of your "fan-tastic" time together. (A fun idea for teen celebrations, when it can be tough to come up with cool birthday party ideas!)

TOMATO BASIL SOUP

Ingredients:
1 Tbsp olive oil
1 fresh tomato, peeled and diced
1 Tbsp celery, diced
1 tsp onion, diced
1 tsp fresh basil
1 Tbsp butter
2 Tbsp flour
1 cup whole milk

Toppings:
1 Tbsp sour cream
Salt and pepper to taste

Directions:
In a skillet, sauté the tomato, celery and onion in the olive oil until tender. Let the vegetables cool slightly, then add the basil. Process the mixture in a food processor or blend until smooth. Meanwhile, melt the butter in the skillet and add the flour, stirring until flour is completely mixed in with the butter. Cook, stirring for another minute or two. Gradually add in the milk, stirring until smooth. Stir in the tomato mixture and ladle into a soup mug. Microwave for a minute to blend the flavors and heat through. Before serving, season with salt and pepper to taste, and top each mug of soup with a dollop of sour cream.

Chili, Chowder & Soup Mugs

CREAMY FRENCH ONION SOUP

Ingredients:
2 Tbsp butter
1/2 onion, sliced into rings
2 Tbsp flour
1/2 cup beef broth
1/4 cup cream
1 slice French bread
Olive oil
1/4 cup Swiss cheese, finely shredded

Directions:
In a medium skillet, sauté the onion rings in the butter until tender and browned around the edges. Remove onions and set aside. Add the flour to the remaining butter, stirring until it is completely mixed together. Gradually add the broth, stirring it into the flour and butter. Turn the heat off and stir in the cream. Add the onions back in and pour into a large oven-proof soup mug. Turn the broiler on to preheat. Brush the bread on both sides with olive oil and cut into fourths. Toast the bread under the broiler on both sides. Place the bread on top of the soup and sprinkle the cheese on top. Place the mug under the broiler until cheese is melted and slightly browned. (Watch carefully—it may just take seconds.)

Chili, Chowder & Soup Mugs

SOUTHWESTERN TACO SOUP

Ingredients:
1/2 lb ground beef
1/4 cup onion, diced
2 tsp taco seasoning
1/4 cup tomato sauce
1/4 cup diced tomatoes, drained
1-2 Tbsp black beans, drained and rinsed
1-2 Tbsp white shoepeg corn
1 Tbsp salsa
1 cup chicken broth
2 Tbsp Monterey Jack cheese, grated
Sour cream (optional)
Chives (optional)

Directions:
Preheat oven to 350°. In a skillet over medium heat brown
the beef with the onion until cooked through, dicing and
crumbling the meat as it cooks. Add the seasoning and tomato
sauce and then stir in the tomatoes, beans, corn and salsa.
Cook over low heat for about 5 minutes. Add the chicken broth
and cook 5 more minutes. Ladle into a soup mug and sprinkle
cheese on top. Microwave for 45 seconds or until cheese is
melted. Add a dollop of sour cream and a sprinkling of chives
to the top before serving.

BROCCOLI CHEESE SOUP

Ingredients:
1 Tbsp onion, chopped fine
1 tsp butter
1/2 cup fresh broccoli, chopped small
1/2 cup chicken broth
1 Tbsp cream cheese
3/4 cup whole milk
1/4 cup Cheddar cheese, finely shredded
Salt and pepper

Directions:
In a large size soup mug, microwave the butter and onion for 1 minute or until onion is tender (times will vary depending on the microwave). Add the broccoli and chicken broth and microwave for 3 minutes until broccoli is cooked as desired. Add the cream cheese, milk, and Cheddar cheese. Continue cooking in the microwave, stirring every 30 seconds or until cheeses are melted and milk is hot. Salt and pepper to taste.

ITALIAN SAUSAGE SOUP

Ingredients:
1/3 cup pasta, cooked and drained
1/4 cup spicy Italian sausage
1 Tbsp green pepper, diced
1 Tbsp onion, diced
2/3 cup tomato sauce
1/4 cup diced tomatoes, drained
2/3 cup chicken broth
1/4 cup mozzarella cheese, shredded

Directions:
Crumble and cook the sausage in a medium skillet, adding in the green pepper and onion about half-way through. Drain off the grease. Measure the tomato sauce, tomatoes, and chicken broth into a soup mug. Spoon the cooked pasta and the sausage mixture into the mug, stir to combine. Sprinkle the cheese on top. Microwave for 1 minute or until cheese is melted.

This is a great way to use up small portions of leftover pasta.

DOUBLE CHEESEBURGER SLIDER

Ingredients:
1/4-1/2 cup ground beef
2 small slices of cheese, your choice
1 small dinner roll
Condiments

Directions:
Divide the meat into two equal parts. Shape into two small round hamburgers that will fit flat into a mug. Place one small hamburger into the mug and place cheese on top of it. Then place the second hamburger and second cheese slice on top. Microwave for 1 minute, 30 seconds and then check to see if the meat is cooked through, but not overcooked. If it is still very pink, cook it a bit longer. Remove the cheeseburgers and serve on the small bun with your favorite condiments.

Comfort Food For You!

So many of these recipes make a welcome one-dish cup of comfort for someone needing a little R & R. Make up the chicken pot pie, for example, and take this healthy lunch to a new mom, a homebound senior, or someone recuperating from an illness.

CHICKEN POT-PIE

Ingredients:
1 cup instant noodles
1 cup water
1/2 cup chicken breast, cooked and cut into bite sized pieces
2 Tbsp peas
1 Tbsp butter
1 Tbsp onion, chopped
2 Tbsp carrots, chopped
1 Tbsp flour
1 cup chicken broth
Salt and pepper to taste
Dough for 1 round of pie crust or 1 large refrigerated biscuit

Directions:
Preheat oven to 350°. Place the noodles and water in a mug and microwave on high for 3-4 minutes until noodles are al dente and water is mostly absorbed. Cook longer if needed. Add the chicken and peas to the noodles. In a small skillet, melt the butter. Add the onion and carrots and sauté 3-4 minutes until tender. Add the flour, stirring to blend completely. Stir in the chicken broth gradually and then pour the broth mixture into the mug of noodles and chicken.

Cut out a round of the crust slightly bigger than the top of the mug or use 1 large biscuit, stretched flat. Place on top of the mug and press firmly down around the rim. Bake in the oven for 10-12 minutes or until biscuit is golden brown.

MEATLOAF FOR ONE

Ingredients:
1/2 cup ground beef
2 Tbsp quick cooking oats
1 Tbsp Worcestershire sauce
2 tsp hot sauce
1 Tbsp green onion, chopped fine
1-2 Tbsp ketchup

Directions:
Spray the inside of a mug with non-stick cooking spray. Combine all ingredients except ketchup. Press into the mug. Cook in the microwave 4 minutes or until meat is no longer pink (times will vary depending on the microwave). Spoon ketchup on the top. Let sit for 2 minutes before removing from mug—or eat it right out of the mug (drain off the juices first).

FLIP-IT-OVER PIZZA

Ingredients:
2 Tbsp pizza sauce
1/2 cup mozzarella cheese
Pizza toppings of your choice (pepperoni slices, black olives, green pepper, Italian sausage)
1 tube of refrigerated pizza crust dough

Directions:
Preheat the oven to 375°. Spoon the sauce into a mug and top it with the cheese. Layer on your favorite pizza toppings. Roll out the pizza crust and cut out a circle a bit bigger than the top of the mug. Lay the dough on the top of the mug, pressing down around the rim. Bake in the oven for 20 minutes or until golden brown. To serve, loosen the crust around the rim of the mug. Carefully flip the mug upside-down onto a plate.

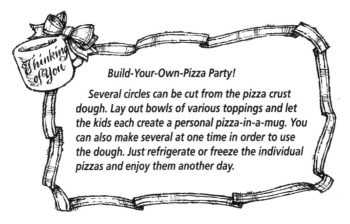

Build-Your-Own-Pizza Party!

Several circles can be cut from the pizza crust dough. Lay out bowls of various toppings and let the kids each create a personal pizza-in-a-mug. You can also make several at one time in order to use the dough. Just refrigerate or freeze the individual pizzas and enjoy them another day.

CLASSIC TUNA CASSEROLE

Ingredients:
1/2 cup quick cook noodles
1 cup water
1 Tbsp cream cheese, softened
1 Tbsp peas
1 Tbsp butter
1/4 cup mushrooms
1 Tbsp flour
1/2 cup chicken broth
1/2 5-oz can tuna, drained, or your choice of fish
1 Tbsp potato chips, crushed

Directions:
Place the noodles and water in a large mug and bring to a boil in the microwave. Cook for 3 minutes or until the noodles are al dente. Drain the water. While the noodles are hot, add the cream cheese and peas to the mug. In a small skillet, melt the butter and sauté the mushrooms. Add the flour, stirring to coat mushrooms. Gradually add the chicken broth and stir until thick and bubbly. Add in the tuna. Pour the tuna/mushroom mixture over the noodles and peas, stirring to combine. Microwave for 1-2 minutes until hot all the way through. When almost done, top with crushed potato chips and finish heating.

Main Dish Mugs

BROCCOLI, CHICKEN AND RICE

Ingredients:
1/3 cup instant rice
1/2 cup chicken broth
1/4 cup cooked broccoli, cut into small pieces
1/2 cup cooked chicken, cut into small pieces
1 Tbsp butter
Salt and pepper to taste

Directions:
Combine all ingredients in a large mug and cook in the micro-wave for 2 minutes or until rice is tender.

What a quick and easy way to make leftovers into a tasty meal! Enjoy it at home, or take it to work for lunch.

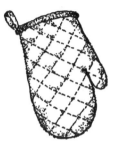

BURGER AND BEANS DINNER

Ingredients:
1/2 cup ground beef, crumbled and cooked
1/2 cup pork and beans
2 slices of bacon, cooked and cut into bite size pieces
1 Tbsp brown sugar
1 Tbsp onion, diced fine
1 Tbsp Cheddar cheese, shredded
1 refrigerated large size biscuit (from a tube)

Directions:
Preheat oven to 400°. Combine all ingredients except biscuit in a large mug. Set the biscuit on top of the hamburger mixture in the mug and place in the oven. Bake for 15-20 minutes or until biscuit is golden brown.

CHICKEN CHILE RELLENO

Ingredients:
1/4 cup sourdough bread, cut into cubes
2 Tbsp diced green chiles, drained and patted dry
2 Tbsp frozen corn, thawed and patted dry
1 scallion, thinly sliced
1-2 Tbsp cooked chicken breast, cut into small pieces
1/4 cup milk
1 large egg white
1 large egg
Dash of salt
1/4 cup Cheddar cheese, finely shredded, divided
2 Tbsp tomato sauce
Sour cream

Directions:
Spray the inside of a mug with non-stick cooking spray. Put the bread, green chiles, corn, scallion, and chicken in the mug. Whisk milk, egg white, egg and salt in a medium bowl until combined, and pour over mug mixture. Top with half the cheese. Microwave for 1 minute, 20 seconds or until egg is done. Spoon the tomato sauce on top, then the remaining shredded cheese, and microwave again for 30 seconds to warm. Serve with a garnish of sour cream.

HAMBURGER NOODLE DISH

Ingredients:
1/2 cup ground beef
1 Tbsp onion, chopped
1/2 tsp garlic
1/4 cup tomato sauce
1 package dried noodle soup
2 Tbsp cream cheese, softened
1/4 cup sour cream
1/4 cup Monterey Jack cheese, shredded

Directions:
In a small skillet, brown the beef with onion and garlic. Add tomato sauce and simmer for about 5 minutes. Meanwhile, cook the noodles in boiling water for 3 minutes. Drain off the water when done. In a small bowl combine the cream cheese and sour cream until smooth. Put half of the noodles in a mug. Next, layer half the meat sauce, then half the sour cream sauce. Repeat layers and top with grated cheese. Microwave for 2 minutes or until heated through and cheese is melted.

Main Dish Mugs

THAI CHICKEN AND VEGETABLES
(RECIPE IS FOR 2 MUGS)

Ingredients:
1 Tbsp olive oil
2 boneless skinless chicken thighs
1/4 cup coconut milk
1/2 cup chicken broth
1/2 cup quick cooking rice, uncooked
1 tsp Thai red curry paste
1/4 cup red bell pepper
1/4 cup yellow bell pepper
1/4 cup green beans

Directions:
In a small skillet heat the olive oil and cook the chicken thighs until well-browned on both sides. Remove from heat and cut into bite size pieces. Add coconut milk, broth, rice, curry paste, and vegetables to a large mug and cook in the microwave for 2 minutes. Add the chicken and cook for 30 seconds longer or until rice is tender.

You can also use leftover cooked chicken to make this meal-in-a-mug in under 5 minutes! Voila!

MUG OF ENCHILADAS

Ingredients:
1 flour tortilla
1/4 cup chicken, cooked and shredded
1/4 cup Monterey Jack cheese, shredded
1 Tbsp butter
1 Tbsp flour
1/4 cup chicken broth
2 Tbsp sour cream
1 Tbsp diced green chiles

Directions:
Spray the inside of a mug with non-stick cooking spray. Tear the tortilla into 1-inch pieces. In a small bowl, combine the chicken and cheese. Layer the tortilla pieces and the chicken mixture into the mug (several layers). In a small skillet, melt the butter, stir in the flour and simmer for one minute, stirring constantly. Gradually add the broth, whisking until smooth. When thickened, add the sour cream and green chiles. Pour the sauce over the chicken and tortillas in the mug. Top with additional shredded cheese if desired. Microwave for 1-2 minutes until cheese has melted.

Main Dish Mugs

HAWAIIAN MEATBALLS IN A MUG

Ingredients:
1 Tbsp brown sugar
1 Tbsp ketchup
2 tsp soy sauce
1/2 tsp garlic, minced
1/2 tsp ginger, minced
4-5 precooked frozen meatballs, thawed
1 Tbsp olive oil
1/4 cup green bell pepper, seeded and cut in pieces
1 Tbsp onion, chopped
1/4 cup pineapple, cut in chunks
1/2 cup beef broth
1 Tbsp honey
1 Tbsp white wine vinegar

Directions:
Mix together in a mug the brown sugar, ketchup, soy sauce, garlic and ginger. Microwave on high for 30 seconds. Place the meatballs in the mug. In a skillet, heat the olive oil and add the bell peppers, onion, and pineapple to sauté. When the vegetables are tender, add the broth, honey and vinegar. Pour the vegetable mixture and sauce over the meatballs and micro-wave for 1-2 minutes, until meatballs are heated through.

Main Dish Mugs

TETRAZZINI IN A MUG

Ingredients:
3/4 cup angel hair pasta, broken into short pieces,
    approx. 1 1/2 inches
3/4 cup water
1/8 tsp salt
1/2 cup half and half
Dash of nutmeg
2 Tbsp mushrooms, sliced
1/4 cup Monterey Jack cheese, shredded
1/4 cup sharp Cheddar cheese, shredded, plus more for topping
Salt and pepper to taste
1/4 cup sweet Italian sausage
1/2 clove of garlic, finely minced
1 sprig of fresh thyme
1/2 tsp of butter

Directions:
Place the pasta pieces in a microwave-safe bowl or large mug. Add water and salt, then stir to combine. Cover the bowl and microwave on high for 4 minutes, then stir again with a fork. Cover and microwave on high again for another minute or two or until the pasta is al dente and the water is absorbed. Add the half and half, nutmeg, mushrooms, and cheeses. Mix evenly and season with salt and pepper. Set aside. Place the Italian sausage, minced garlic, thyme and butter into an extra large mug. Mix them slightly, then microwave on high for 1 minute. Break up the sausage meat with a fork and return to the microwave for another minute. Drain out any grease that might be in the mug. Pour the pasta and cheese mixture into the mug and mix with the sausage on the bottom. Top with more shredded Cheddar and Jack. Microwave on high for 3 minutes or until hot and bubbly.

⣿⣿⣿⣿ Main Dish Mugs ⣿⣿⣿⣿

HAM, ASPARAGUS AND POTATO PIE

Ingredients:
1 Tbsp butter
1 Tbsp onion, diced fine
1 1/2 cups mashed potatoes
1/4 cup cooked ham, cut into bite sized pieces
1/4 cup asparagus, cooked and cut into 1 inch pieces
Salt and pepper to taste
1/2 cup Cheddar cheese, shredded
1/4 cup corn flake cereal, crushed

Directions:
In a large microwave-safe mug, combine butter and onion. Microwave, uncovered, on high for 2 minutes or until tender, stirring once. Add potatoes, ham, asparagus, salt and pepper; mix well. Sprinkle with cheese and corn flakes. Microwave for 1 minute more or until cheese is melted.

Know someone who's homebound and may be missing out on the traditional Easter feast? You can use some of your leftovers to make up this wonderful one-dish dinner to take to them. (And remember to bring the chocolate!)

LOADED POTATO MUG

Ingredients:
Leftover mashed potatoes or instant mashed patatoes
  prepared with milk, water, butter

Toppings:
Chives
Bacon, cooked and crumbled
Cheese, shredded
Sour cream

Directions:
This is perfect for leftover mashed potatoes or you can make
instant mashed potatoes according to the instructions on the
packaging, using milk, water, and butter. Heat the potatoes
for 2 minutes in the microwave on high. Top with your favorite
potato toppings and reheat (if desired) to melt the cheese.

*A great gift for a college student or "welcome
to your first apartment" gift. Give a great set
of his or her first mugs, along with a collection
of easy recipes, including this one.*

MEXICAN CORN CASSEROLE

Ingredients:
1 small egg
1 Tbsp milk
1/2 cup corn muffin mix
1/4 cup Cheddar cheese, divided
1/4 lb ground beef
1 Tbsp onion, diced
1 Tbsp green chiles, diced
1 Tbsp salsa
2 tsp taco seasoning

Toppings:
Sour cream
Salsa

Directions:
Preheat oven to 350°. In a small bowl, whisk the egg and milk together. Add the corn muffin mix and 1/2 of the cheese. Stir until just blended. Set aside. In a small skillet over medium heat, combine the ground beef, onion, green chiles, salsa and taco seasoning. Cook, stirring, until meat is no longer pink. Drain off grease. Spray a large mug with non-stick cooking spray. Spoon 1/2 of the muffin batter into the mug. Spoon the meat mixture on top of the muffin batter. Add the rest of the muffin batter on top of the meat and top with the remaining cheese. Bake in the oven for 15 minutes or until golden brown and a toothpick inserted in the center comes out clean. Serve with sour cream and salsa.

This dish is hearty enough to be a meal-in-one.

Side Mugs

SAUSAGE AND RICE FLORENTINE

Ingredients:
1/2 cup quick cooking rice
1/2 cup water
1/2 cup spinach leaves, chopped or 1/4 cup frozen spinach
1/4 cup Cheddar cheese, shredded
1 small egg, beaten
Dash of Worcestershire sauce
1 Tbsp butter, melted
2 Tbsp milk
1/4 cup Italian sausage, cooked and crumbled
Salt and pepper to taste

Directions:
Place all ingredients into a large mug and stir together. Microwave for 2-4 minutes until rice is tender and water absorbed.

VEGETABLE MEDLEY

Ingredients:
1/2 zucchini, peeled and sliced
1/4 cup corn
1/4 cup fresh tomatoes, diced
1/4 cup yellow squash, peeled and sliced
1 Tbsp butter
Seasoned salt and pepper to taste
1/4 cup butter crackers, crushed

Directions:
Place all the vegetables into a mug with the butter. Salt and pepper to taste. Microwave on high for 1-2 minutes (depending on how you prefer your vegetables). Sprinkle the crushed crackers on top for a garnish.

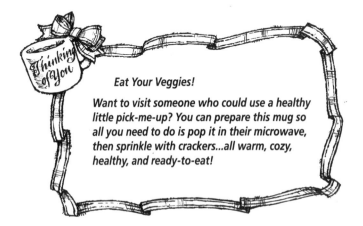

Eat Your Veggies!

Want to visit someone who could use a healthy little pick-me-up? You can prepare this mug so all you need to do is pop it in their microwave, then sprinkle with crackers...all warm, cozy, healthy, and ready-to-eat!

Side Mugs

HOMEMADE MAC AND CHEESE

Ingredients:
3/4 cup dry pasta
1 cup water
1 egg
1/2 cup whole milk
1 Tbsp sour cream
1 Tbsp butter, softened
1/4 cup Cheddar cheese
1/4 cup Swiss cheese
1/4 cup Monterey Jack cheese
1/4 cup butter crackers, crushed (optional)

Directions:
In a large size soup mug stir together the pasta and water.
Microwave on high for 5 minutes. Stir. Continue microwaving, stirring and checking at 30 second intervals until pasta is cooked to desired tenderness and water is mostly absorbed. Add more water if needed and then drain off when pasta is cooked. In a small bowl whisk together the egg, milk, and sour cream. Add the butter and cheeses to the pasta, then pour the milk-egg mixture over all. Microwave for 1-2 minutes and then stir. Continue to microwave until the cheeses are melted. Sprinkle crushed crackers on top if desired.

Side Mugs

SWEET POTATO CASSEROLE

Ingredients:
1 sweet potato, peeled and cut into cubes
1/4 cup milk
1/4 cup brown sugar
1 egg, beaten
1/2 Tbsp butter, melted
1 1/2 tsp cinnamon
1/8 tsp allspice
1/4 tsp salt
1 cup mini marshmallows

Directions:
Preheat the oven to 350°. Put the cubed sweet potatoes in a mug and cover with plastic wrap. Microwave the sweet potatoes until tender, about 1 minute. Using a fork, mash the sweet potatoes until the larger chunks are gone. Add the milk, brown sugar, egg, butter, and spices. Mix well. Place mug in the oven and bake for 5 minutes. Remove from the oven, put the marshmallows on top and put back in the oven. Bake, watching closely, until marshmallows turn golden on the top.

⚶⚶⚶ Cakes, Brownies & Cookie ⚶⚶⚶ Mugs

CHOCOLATE CHIP CHEESECAKE

Ingredients:
1/2 graham cracker, crushed
1 tsp butter, melted
2 Tbsp powdered sugar
2 Tbsp sour cream
3 Tbsp cream cheese
1/4 tsp vanilla extract
1/2 egg, beaten (egg substitute works too)
1 Tbsp mini chocolate chips

Directions:
In a small bowl combine the graham cracker and butter. Press into the bottom of a mug. In another bowl whisk together powdered sugar, sour cream, cream cheese, vanilla extract, and egg until well combined. Stir in the chocolate chips. Pour into the mug. Microwave on high for 1 minute. Open microwave door for 20 seconds, close, and microwave for another minute or until it is set. Remove from microwave, let cool for 10 minutes, then transfer to the fridge for about 2 hours.

Cakes, Brownies & Cookie Mugs

SALTED CARAMEL CAKE

(RECIPE IS FOR 2 MUGS)

Ingredients:
2 Tbsp unsalted butter, softened
1/4 cup granulated sugar
1 large egg
1/2 tsp pure vanilla extract
1 tsp store-bought caramel sauce
2 tsp milk
6 tsp self-rising flour
1/2 tsp high-quality sea salt, divided
4 caramel candies

Directions:
In a large mug, whisk together the butter and sugar with a fork. Stir in the egg, vanilla, caramel sauce and milk. Add the flour and 1/4 teaspoon of the sea salt. Beat the batter until smooth. Divide the batter between two mugs. Top each mug with a pinch of the remaining salt. Microwave separately for 30 seconds each. Top each mug with two caramel candies. Continue cooking 1 to 1 1/2 minutes more (each separately) until cake has risen.

Cakes, Brownies & Cookie Mugs

PECAN CRUMBLE COFFEE CAKE

Ingredients:
1 Tbsp butter, softened
2 Tbsp sugar
1/2 egg, beaten
2 Tbsp applesauce
2 drops vanilla extract
1/4 cup flour
1/8 tsp baking powder

Topping:
2 Tbsp flour
1 Tbsp brown sugar
1 tsp cinnamon
1 Tbsp butter
1 Tbsp pecans, chopped and toasted

Directions:
Stir 1 Tbsp softened butter and sugar together in a coffee mug until fluffy. In a small bowl, whisk together egg, applesauce, and vanilla. Pour egg mixture into the butter mixture. Add 1/4 cup flour and baking powder into the mixture, stirring until smooth. In a separate bowl, mix together 2 Tbsp flour, brown sugar, and cinnamon. Mash 1 Tbsp butter into the flour mixture with a fork or pastry cutter until mixture is crumbly, then stir in the toasted pecans. Sprinkle the topping over the cake batter in mug. Microwave on high for 1 minute. Continue cooking in 10 second intervals until a toothpick inserted into the middle comes out clean.

Cakes, Brownies & Cookie Mugs

CHOCOLATE-MINT CAKE

Ingredients:
5 Tbsp flour
4 Tbsp brown sugar
2 tsp unsweetened cocoa powder
1/4 tsp baking soda
4 tsp whole milk
2 tsp canola oil
1/2 tsp white vinegar
1/4 tsp mint extract
Powdered sugar
1 sprig of mint

Directions:
In a large mug, mix together the flour, brown sugar, cocoa powder and baking soda. Add in the milk, oil, vinegar and mint extract.

Place on high for 2 minutes. Remove from the microwave, and top with powdered sugar and a sprig of mint.

Give this made-in-a-mug cake as a Christmas gift. In place of the fresh mint, top with crushed peppermint candies. Wrap in plastic wrap, tie with ribbon, and attach a candy cane to the gift tag.

∴∴∴∵ Cakes, Brownies & Cookie ∵∴∵∴ Mugs

SWEET CRISPY TREATS

Ingredients:
4-5 large size marshmallows
2 Tbsp butter
1 Tbsp butterscotch chips
1 Tbsp chocolate chips
1 cup crispy rice cereal

Directions:
Spray the inside of a mug with non-stick cooking spray. Put the marshmallows and butter in the mug and microwave for 1 minute or until the marshmallows and butter are melted (time will vary depending on the power of the microwave). Stir together, microwave again for 10-15 seconds and stir again. Stir in the butterscotch and chocolate chips, and then add the cereal. Mix well then pat down in the mug to cool.

A super fun and easy treat to make with kids. Remember the mug will be HOT when removed from microwave, so keep small hands safe.

Cakes, Brownies & Cookie Mugs

BLONDE BROWNIE

Ingredients:
3 Tbsp butter
1 small egg, beaten
1/4 tsp vanilla extract
1/4 cup sugar
1/4 cup flour

Frosting:
1 Tbsp powdered sugar
1 Tbsp butter
1 tsp milk

Directions:
Place the butter in a mug and microwave for 30 seconds or until butter is melted. Swirl butter around in the mug to coat the sides. Break the egg into a small bowl, add vanilla. Whisk the egg until beaten and fluffy. Add the sugar and egg to the butter. Whisk to blend the ingredients. Add the flour, stirring until smooth. Microwave for 1 minute, 20 seconds or until toothpick inserted in center comes out clean. For frosting: mix together 1 Tbsp powdered sugar, 1 Tbsp butter, 1 tsp milk until smooth. Add more milk if needed for consistency. Drizzle frosting on top of the brownie.

Cakes, Brownies & Cookie Mugs

OATS AND APPLESAUCE CAKE

Ingredients:
½ cup old fashioned oats
1 Tbsp flour
1 tsp baking powder
1 tsp vanilla extract
1 tsp sugar
3 Tbsp applesauce, unsweetened
2 Tbsp milk
2 eggs

Frosting:
1/2 cup powdered sugar
3 Tbsp butter, softened
2-4 tsp milk
1/4 tsp vanilla extract

Directions:
Combine all cake ingredients in a bowl, mixing until light and fluffy. Spray a mug with non-stick cooking spray. Pour batter into the mug and microwave on high for 2 minutes. Let cool before frosting. Meanwhile, combine the frosting ingredients. Spread over cake when cooled.

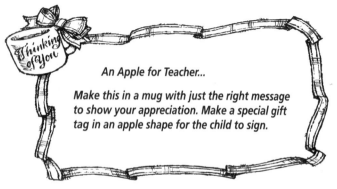

An Apple for Teacher...

Make this in a mug with just the right message to show your appreciation. Make a special gift tag in an apple shape for the child to sign.

Cakes, Brownies & Cookie Mugs

TRES LECHES CAKE

Ingredients:
3 Tbsp whipping cream
3 Tbsp condensed milk
1/4 cup flour
2 Tbsp sugar
1/4 tsp baking soda
1 tsp baking powder
4 Tbsp milk
2 Tbsp canola oil
1 tsp vanilla

Toppings:
Whipped cream
Vanilla ice cream (optional)
Cinnamon-sugar for garnish

Directions:
Whisk the whipping cream together with the condensed milk and set aside. Measure the flour, sugar, baking soda and baking powder into a large mug, stir to combine. Add the milk, oil, and vanilla to the mug and mix them into the dry ingredients until everything is combined. Microwave for 45-90 seconds (depending on the strength of the microwave), or until the cake is puffy and just springs back gently to the touch. Do not overcook. Remove the cake from the microwave and let cool for 3-4 minutes. Poke holes in the cake with a skewer in multiple places, then pour condensed milk/whipping cream mixture over the cake. Serve cake warm with whipped cream or a scoop of vanilla ice cream and a sprinkle of cinnamon-sugar.

Cakes, Brownies & Cookie Mugs

SHORTBREAD MUG CAKE

Ingredients:
2-3 shortbread cookies (store bought or homemade),
    crumbled; divided
2 Tbsp flour
1 Tbsp sugar
1/2 tsp baking powder
1/2 banana, mashed
1 small egg
1/4 cup whole milk
1 tsp coarse sugar

Directions:
Spray a large mug with non-stick cooking spray. Put 1/2 of
the cookie crumbs into the mug. In a small bowl, combine
flour, sugar and baking powder until sifted together. Add the
banana, egg, and milk, stirring to make a smooth batter. Stir in
remaining 1/2 of the cookie crumbs. Spoon the batter into the
mug on top of the cookie crumbs. Bake in the microwave for
1 minute, 20 seconds or until toothpick inserted in center
comes out clean. Sprinkle 1 tsp coarse sugar on top before
serving.

⁂ Cakes, Brownies & Cookie Mugs

EASY CHOCOLATE PEANUT BUTTER BROWNIE

Ingredients:
2 Tbsp butter, softened
2 Tbsp sugar
1 1/2 Tbsp brown sugar
1 egg
1 Tbsp cocoa powder
3 Tbsp flour
Pinch of salt
1 piece chocolate peanut butter cup candy

Directions:
Mix together the butter, sugar, brown sugar, and egg until smooth. Stir in the cocoa, flour and salt until well combined. Pour half of the batter into the mug, set the piece of choco-late-peanut butter candy on the top, and then cover it with the rest of the batter. Microwave for 45-75 seconds. Check often—don't over cook.

Easter is a great time to make up this simple treat, with the yummy taste of a peanut butter cup surprise hidden inside.

✳✳✳ Cakes, Brownies & Cookie ✳✳✳ Mugs

CHOCOLATE CHIP SURPRISE

Ingredients:
1 roll of refrigerated chocolate chip cookie dough
2 oz cream cheese
1 egg, beaten
1 Tbsp sugar

Directions:
Preheat oven to 350°. Press 1 slice of cookie dough into the bottom of an oven safe mug. In a small bowl, mix together the cream cheese, egg and sugar. Spread the cream cheese mixture on top of the cookie dough. Put another slice of cookie dough on top.

Bake in the oven for 12-15 minutes. Let cool before indulging (if you can wait).

Yummy fun to make with little ones!

Cakes, Brownies & Cookie Mugs

BERRIES AND CREAM CAKE

Ingredients:
1 Tbsp butter, softened
1 egg
1 Tbsp milk
1 tsp vanilla
1 1/2 Tbsp sugar
2 Tbsp flour

1/8 tsp baking powder
Dash of salt
1/4 cup cream
1 Tbsp powdered sugar
1 Tbsp berry preserves
2 Tbsp fresh or frozen mixed berries

Directions:
Microwave the butter in a mug until melted, about 15 seconds. In a small bowl, whisk together the egg, milk, and vanilla until well blended. Add the sugar, flour, baking powder, and salt and whisk again until the batter is smooth. Microwave for 1 minute, 10 seconds or until cake is set, (If not done, return to microwave for up to 20 seconds more, checking after 10 seconds.) Set aside to cool. Meanwhile, whisk together the cream and powdered sugar until gentle peaks form. Spoon the preserves over the cake, then the whipped cream, and top with the berries.

Beautiful and elegant, a great treat when the harvest is in, and sweet summer berries are at their best.

Cakes, Brownies & Cookie Mugs

BROWNIE SUNDAE IN A MUG

Ingredients:

2 Tbsp butter, softened	4 Tbsp flour
2 Tbsp sugar	1/4 tsp baking powder
1 Tbsp brown sugar	2 Tbsp mini chocolate chips, divided
1 Tbsp cocoa powder	Vanilla ice cream
1 egg	Chocolate syrup
1/2 tsp vanilla	

Directions:

Melt the butter in a mug—about 15 seconds in the microwave. Add the sugars and cocoa to the butter and stir well. Add the egg and vanilla, then the flour and baking powder, making sure it is completely mixed. Add half of the chocolate chips to the batter. Microwave for about 45-50 seconds. Remove from the microwave and top with the rest of the chocolate chips. Microwave for another 30 seconds. Let cool. Serve with a scoop of vanilla ice cream and a drizzle of chocolate syrup.

Every Dae is a Fun Dae—
when you add this SUNDAE!

Congratulate a deserving graduate, cheer up someone who needs a lift, or honor a birthday person. Add a balloon, ribbon, or note to this mug and deliver it to the person. Don't forget to say "add ice cream".

Pies, Puddings & Custard Mugs

LEMON SOUFFLÉ

Ingredients:
1/4 cup sugar
2 1/2 tsp flour
1/8 tsp salt
1 small egg, separated
1/4 cup milk
1 1/2 tsp fresh lemon juice
2 tsp butter, melted

Directions:
Preheat oven to 450°. Spray an oven-safe mug with non-stick cooking spray. Combine the sugar, flour, and salt in a small bowl. Add the egg yolk, milk, lemon juice, and butter. In a separate bowl, with an electric mixer, beat the egg white until stiff peaks form. Fold the egg white into the batter. Bake for 5 minutes at 450° and then reduce the oven temperature to 375°. Bake for another 10-15 minutes or until soufflé puffs up and the top turns golden.

Pies, Puddings & Custard Mugs

BAKED CUSTARD MUG

Ingredients:
1 egg
5 tsp sugar
1/8 tsp salt
1/2 cup milk
1/8 tsp vanilla
Dash of nutmeg

Directions:
Preheat oven to 350°. Spray the inside of an oven-safe mug with non-stick cooking spray. In a small bowl, combine and beat together the egg, sugar, and salt. Pour the milk into a microwave-safe glass bowl or measuring cup. Microwave the milk until it starts to boil. Let the hot milk cool slightly, then very carefully remove the boiling milk from the microwave. Let milk cool until lukewarm. Stir the egg mixture into the milk. Add the vanilla. Pour into oven-safe mug. Sprinkle a dash of nutmeg on top of the custard and then bake for 30 minutes in the oven or until knife inserted in center comes out clean.

Pies, Puddings & Custard Mugs

KEY LIME MUG PIE

Ingredients:
1 tsp lime zest
1 egg yolk
1 1/2 Tbsp lime juice
1/2 cup sweetened condensed milk
2 graham crackers, crushed
1 Tbsp butter
1/2 cup whipped cream
1 to 3 tsp sugar

Directions:
Preheat oven to 325°. Spray the inside of an oven-safe mug with non-stick cooking spray. In a small bowl, whisk together the lime zest and egg yolk. Add the lime juice, and condensed milk. Set aside. Put the graham cracker crumbs and butter in a mug and microwave for 30 seconds or until butter melts. Stir until completely combined. Press against the bottom and sides of the mug to form a crust. Spoon the filling into the mug and bake in the oven for 5-8 minutes or until slightly set. Remove from oven and chill. Whip the cream, adding sugar a little at a time, to desired sweetness. Top the pie with whipped cream before serving.

Pies, Puddings & Custard Mugs

CREAMY RICE PUDDING

Ingredients:
1 cup milk
1/2 cup half and half or cream
1 egg
1/2 tsp vanilla
1/2 cup cooked rice
2 Tbsp sugar
1/4 cup dried cranberries
1/8 tsp salt
1 pat of butter
Cinnamon
Nutmeg

Directions:
Whisk together in a small bowl the milk, half and half, egg, and vanilla. Combine the milk/egg mixture with the rice, sugar, cranberries and salt in a mug, stirring well. Microwave on high for 3 minutes. Let sit for 1 minute. Put a pat of butter on top and sprinkle with a dash of cinnamon and nutmeg if desired.

PUMPKIN CRUMBLE

Filling:
1/2 cup pumpkin puree
2 Tbsp sugar
1 tsp pumpkin pie spice
1 egg, beaten
1 Tbsp evaporated milk

Crumble Topping:
1 Tbsp flour
2 Tbsp brown sugar
1/4 tsp salt
1/2 tsp cinnamon
2 Tbsp butter
1 Tbsp oatmeal
1 Tbsp chopped pecans
Sweetened whipped cream (optional)

Directions:
For the filling: Mix all ingredients in a mug. For the topping, combine the first four topping ingredients in a bowl, then cut in the butter with a pastry blender or food processor until crumble is pea-sized. Stir in oatmeal and pecans. Spread the crumble on top of the pumpkin pie filling, microwave for 2-3 minutes or until filling is slightly set. Let cool for a few minutes before serving with a dollop of sweetened whipped cream.

Pies, Puddings & Custard Mugs

CHERRY PRETZEL PIE IN A MUG

Ingredients:
1/4 cup crushed pretzels
2 Tbsp melted butter
1 Tbsp sugar
1 oz cream cheese, softened
1 cup sugar
1/4 cup store-bought frozen whipped cream topping
1/4 cup cherry pie filling

Directions:
Preheat oven to 350°. Mix crushed pretzels, melted butter and 1 Tbsp sugar; press into bottom of an oven safe mug. Bake for 8 minutes. Cool. Combine cream cheese with 1 cup sugar until well mixed. Stir in frozen whipped topping. Spread cream cheese mixture on pretzel crust. Spoon cherry pie filling on top. Refrigerate.

Munchie Mugs

LAYERED NACHO DIP

Ingredients:
1/4 cup refried beans
1 Tbsp green chiles, diced
2 Tbsp tomato, diced and seeded
1 Tbsp onion, diced
1/4 cup Cheddar cheese, shredded
2 Tbsp sour cream
1-2 tsp taco seasoning
Black olives
Avocado
Salsa
Tortilla chips

Directions:
Mix together the refried beans and green chiles. Spoon into the bottom of a short, flat-bottomed mug. Sprinkle the tomatoes and onion on the beans. Next, spread on a layer of Cheddar cheese. Place mug into the microwave and cook on high until cheese is melted, about 45 seconds. Mix together the sour cream and taco seasoning, then spread on top of the melted cheese. Layer on the rest of the ingredients and serve with tortilla chips.

BAKED EGG BLT

Ingredients:
1/2 ripe avocado
2 slices of a ripe tomato
2 slices bacon, cooked
1 egg
Salt & pepper, to taste
2 pieces bread
1 Tbsp light mayonnaise
2 sandwich sized lettuce leaves

Directions:
Preheat the oven to 350°. Spray the inside of an oven-safe mug with non-stick cooking spray. A short, wide mug or a soup mug works well for this recipe. Cut the avocado in half, remove pit, and slice lengthwise. With a large spoon, scoop it gently out of its peeling so that the slices stay intact. Set the avocado slices in the mug, fanning out slightly. Put the tomato slices on top of the avocado and then the bacon slices. Carefully crack the egg on top of all, trying not to break yolk. Sprinkle salt and pepper on top. Bake for 20-30 minutes until egg reaches desired doneness. When the egg is nearly done, toast the bread and spread with mayonnaise. Place the lettuce leaves on the bread. After removing the mug from the oven, carefully turn it over onto the lettuce and place the other piece of toast on top. Serve warm. A bit messy...but a lot tasty!

Munchie Mugs

BROWN SUGAR APPLES

Ingredients:
1 tart apple
1 Tbsp dried cranberries
1 Tbsp brown sugar
1 Tbsp flour
1 Tbsp butter
1 Tbsp pecans, chopped

Directions:
Core and dice the apple and put in a mug. Add the cranberries. In a small bowl combine the brown sugar, flour, butter, and pecans, stirring until it becomes crumbly. Sprinkle the crumble over the apples and bake in the microwave for 2-3 minutes or until apple is tender.

PB & J SNACK

Ingredients:
2 graham crackers, crushed
1 Tbsp butter, melted
2 oz cream cheese, softened
2-3 Tbsp chunky peanut butter
2 Tbsp sugar
1 1/2 tsp milk
1 tsp honey
1 8-oz container frozen whipped topping
2 Tbsp jelly or fruit preserves

Directions:
Combine the crushed graham crackers and melted butter in a mug. Stir together until completely combined. Remove about a tablespoon to sprinkle on the top. Using your fingers, press against the bottom and sides of the mug. In a bowl, mix together the cream cheese, peanut butter, sugar, milk, and honey. Add the whipped topping and mix well. Spoon into the mug. Stir the jelly, adding a teaspoon of water to thin slightly. Drizzle the jelly on top and sprinkle with reserved graham cracker crumbs. Chill or freeze before serving.

Munchie Mugs

CHOCOLATE CHIP BANANA BREAD

Ingredients:
1 small ripe banana, mashed
1 Tbsp canola oil
1 small egg
1 Tbsp milk
4 Tbsp brown sugar
4 Tbsp flour
1/4 tsp baking powder
1 Tbsp chocolate chips
Powdered sugar

Directions:
Mix together in a mug the mashed banana, oil, egg, and milk. Add the brown sugar, flour, and baking powder. Beat well until smooth. Fold in the chocolate chips. Microwave on high for 2-3 minutes (depending on the microwave). Sprinkle with powdered sugar when cool.